T0196008

Does The BAPTISM Of The HOLY SPIRIT Belong in Today's Church?

DR. ROD EAST

authorHOUSE®

AuthorHouse™
1663 Liberty Drive
Bloomington, IN 47403
www.authorhouse.com
Phone: 1 (800) 839-8640

Published by AuthorHouse 01/03/2020

ISBN: 978-1-7283-4148-4 (sc)
ISBN: 978-1-7283-4149-1 (e)

Print information available on the last page.

CONTENTS

PREFACE

The answer to that question is yes! And it is my task and obligation to clarify this stand by using the Word of God, King James Version, and the reference books that support that translation, New American Standard Version, and my life experiences as a Christian and a Pastor. These will be my primary resources.

It would behoove the reader of this thesis to review the "Clarification of Terms", so we have the same understanding, because I have found that my understanding of a term can mean something different to the person who is reading it.

Allow the Holy Spirit to minister to your spirit as you read this information on the Baptism of the Holy Spirit[1], for the Holy Spirit will speak only what he hears from God the Father.[2]

---

[1] I Corinthians 2: 13 (NASB)

[2] John 16: 13(NIV)

Clarification of Terms

Baptism of the Holy Spirit in the Charismatic Movement and in the Pentecostal Movement or any other movement of God is the same baptism that happened at the day of Pentecost, like the gift of Salvation, you have to receive the gift of Jesus' Baptism of the Holy Spirit by faith.[3]

Fast is just that. No food; no liquids, unless you become dehydrated, then water only. Nothing enters the stomach. The purpose for fasting is to show repentance and humility before the Lord and you are earnestly seeking His will in your life, singularly or as a group.

Holy Spirit is the very essence of God; for God is spirit. [4]The Holy Spirit and Holy Ghost are the same.

Slain in the Spirit is a term that is used to explain the filling of the Holy Spirit to the point where your flesh cannot stand under the power of the Spirit and your body falls to the ground without injury. ((There are a lot of opinions out, including mine (Mine will be discussed in Chapter 4.), which agree or disagree that this phenomenon is of God or that it is good or bad.))

---

[3] Hebrew 13: 8 (NIV)

[4] John 4: 24 a (NASB

Speaking in new tongues in reference to the scriptures,

Mark 16: 17 NASB, implies, as Disciples of Christ, that we speak in a new tongue. The reference book I used "Young's Analytical Concordance of the Bible", by Robert Young. The word "new[5]" means just that. However when you look the word up in "The New Strong's Expanded Dictionary of Bible Words", by James Strong, LL.D., S.T.D., says that the new tongue [6]was only new to the speaker and not new to man's hearing. I disagree with that; because, if God can give people a different (New) tongue to speak at the Tower of Babel, in Babylon[7], then he can give us a new language allowing us to only speak to God, spirit to Spirit; for self-edification and for prophecy by interpretation. I am not saying that the Holy Spirit cannot minister in tongues in a known language (The Holy Spirit did so at the day of Pentecost) for the person or persons who is hearing it for their salvation, but for this thesis we are going with the fore mentioned definition. Who are we to limit God?

---

[5] Young's Analytical Concordance to the Bible – Page 694, 06.

[6] The New Strong's Expanded Dictionary of Bible Words – Page 1158, *2538* (02)

[7] Genesis 11: 4 – 9 (NASB)

CHAPTER 01

ENTER THE HOLY SPIRIT

(The Comforter)

Before Jesus ascended into heaven he told his disciples to wait in Jerusalem to be endued [8]with the power of the Holy Spirit[9]. Then on the day of Pentecost they were gathered in one accord and they were baptized in the Holy Spirit. They were speaking in other tongues as the Holy Ghost gave them utterance. (We see that the Holy Spirit was and is always in control of the gift of tongues.) [10]You were able to see the physical effect of the Baptism of the Holy Spirit, for some who saw them, this phenomenon going on, thought that they were drunk. [11]This initial empowering of the Holy Spirit enabled Peter to give his first

---

[8] Young's Analytical Concordance to the Bible – Page 299, 2. Be clothed with.

[9] Luke 24: 49 (KJV)

[10] Acts 2: 1 – 4 (NASB)

[11] Acts 2: 13 (NIV)

Holy Spirit filled sermon. (The start of Peter's ministry.) And over three thousand people received Christ that day[12]. The church did not move forward until it had received the baptism of the Holy Spirit. That in its self should be sufficient basis for the need of the Baptism of the Holy Spirit in today's church.

We will move on, however, to the next case in point. Cornelius had a house full of Gentiles that believed in God and as Peter spoke to them about the good news of Jesus Christ, all of them that heard the word were baptized in the Holy Spirit, with the evidence of speaking in tongues.[13] In this instance all that was needed to receive the Baptism of the Holy Spirit was hearing the Good News. Granted there was prayer and fasting going on beforehand, but hearing the Word of God, which produces faith [14]was the catalyst. The interesting thing about this encounter of the Holy Spirit is that the people in this instance received the Baptism of the Holy Spirit before they had received water baptism. This also shows that whoever believes in Jesus Christ can receive the Baptism of the Holy Spirit. Also God thought that it was important enough for this group of believers to receive the Baptism of the Holy Spirit that he had to teach Peter that it was

---

[12] Acts 2: 14 – 41 (NASB)

[13] Acts 10: 34 – 48 (NASB)

[14] Romans 10: 17

okay to associate with other believers other than Jewish believers[15], and to show that the Holy Spirit is still in control.

I will share what a good friend shared with me on his Baptism of the Holy Spirit. The day that he was baptized in water he was also baptized in the Holy Spirit; for when he came up out of the water he was speaking in tongues. Showing you can receive the Baptism of the Holy Spirit anyway God sees fit. This again confirms the need for the Baptism of the Holy Spirit in the church today.

The next passage that continues to confirm the need of the Baptism of the Holy Spirit is when the saints are gathered together to pray after personal testimony of the Apostles. They came together in prayer in one accord and the place where they had gathered was shaken and they were all baptized in the Holy Spirit to empower them to share the good news with boldness.[16]

God showed the need for his people to be baptized by the Holy Spirit to give them the power and spiritual boldness they needed to be witnesses of Christ that they could share the good news according to God's Holy Spirit.

Another example of someone receiving the Baptism of the Holy Spirit is found in the book of Acts. Saul (Paul) meets Jesus

---

[15] Acts 10: 9 – 20 (NASB

[16] Acts 4: 23 – 31 (NASB)

on the way to Damascus and becomes blind during the event and is lead to Judas' house on Straight Street, where Jesus told Ananias to go and lay hands on Saul, so he could receive his healing, and be filled (Spiritual Baptism) with the Holy Spirit.[17]

We see in this instance that the Baptism of The Holy Spirit was received through the laying on of hands. Now Paul was a Pharisee and was very knowledgeable (Mans understanding) about the Law of Moses and God's Word under the old Covenant as well as man's traditions. But we see Jesus required that he be filled with the Holy Spirit so he could have revelation knowledge of what he was taught by man. Paul considered that all the teaching he received from man as rubbish. [18]Through the Holy Spirit of God, Paul received the deep revelation of God and Peter in his own writings concurs with this fact.[19]

When the Apostles heard that the people in Samaria had received the word of God they sent Peter and John to pray for them to receive the Baptism of the Holy Spirit. They laid hands upon them and they received the Baptism of the Holy Spirit. [20]The laying on of hands is the most common practice to receive the Baptism of the Holy Spirit in today's church, but it is not all

---

[17] Acts 9: 1 – 18 (NASB)

[18] Philippians 3: 4 – 9 (KJV)

[19] II Peter 3: 15 & 16 (NASB)

[20] Acts 8: 14 – 17 (NASB)

inclusive to the act of receiving the Baptism of the Holy Spirit, for God, Jesus Christ, still distributes his Spirit as he sees fit.

We see during Peter's first sermon that he refers to the prophet Joel's writing that in the last days God was and is pouring out his Spirit on all people both men and women, so they can give prophecy, young men can see visions and old men will dream dreams[21]. We continue in these last days (The last days beginning at the day of Pentecost and continuing to this day.) to receive the pouring out of God's Holy Spirit.

The final case in point I have to offer is Jesus 'Baptism of the Holy Spirit. The day Jesus received the baptism of John (Water baptism); Jesus also receives the Baptism of the Holy Spirit from His Father in Heaven.[22]We do not see Jesus move out into His ministry until He receives the Baptism of the Holy Spirit. And Jesus being our perfect example shows us that not only are we to be baptized in water; we are, also, to be baptized in God's Holy Spirit! Because even though Jesus was the Word of God manifested in the flesh He was still 100% human needing to be empowered by the Holy Spirit to do the will of His Father.

In summary we see that the church was jump-started at the day of Pentecost. That the whole church (the body of Christ) needs

---

[21] Acts 2: 14 – 18 (NASB)

[22] Matthew 3: 13 – 17 (NASB)

to be baptized by the Holy Spirit and individuals can be baptized with the laying on of hands, but the body of Christ can receive the Baptism of the Holy Spirit any way God sees fit. Being baptized in the Holy Spirit does not have to come in any particular order as long as you belong to Christ. We receive this pouring out of God's Spirit so we can present the good news of Jesus Christ in spiritual boldness and power and with God's wisdom and understanding; for it is impossible to do it on our own. Jesus being our perfect example shows our need for Spiritual baptism as well as water baptism.

The mention of speaking in tongues in association with being baptized in the Holy Spirit is prevalent in the Book of Acts and we saw earlier in the terms section, as Disciples we speak in a new tongue. Therefore we need to understand what speaking in tongues is about and this spiritual gift in relationship to today's church.

CHAPTER 02

SPEAKING IN A NEW TONGUE!

Speaking in an unknown tongue (Not known to the speaker) is probably the most controversial gift known to mankind. It is not only controversial, but it is probably the most miss-understood and most miss-used gift of God given to man. God foreknew this would become a problem for He had Paul devote an entire chapter to the gift of tongues and prophecy (Apparently we would have a problem with Prophecy too.) and their relationship to each other and to Christ's church.

To receive a better understanding of what the gift of tongues is all about we need to review I Corinthians Chapter 14 and we will start with the first four verses. Paul starts out, vs. 1 – 4, by saying we should <u>earnestly</u>[23] seek or <u>desire</u> [24]spiritual gifts and the most important gift being prophecy. Paul continues to

---

[23] NASB

[24] KJV

say when someone speaks in tongues they are not speaking to man, but to God. Because <u>no man</u> understands what is being said, but the person who speaks through his spirit, via the Holy Spirit, speaks mysteries to God. However, the person who is prophesying is speaking to man for their edification, exhortation, and consolation [25] or <u>comfort</u>[26]. Paul then concludes with the one who is speaking in an unknown tongue is edifying one's self, while the one who is prophesying is edifying the Body of Christ, the Church.

In the next fifteen verses, vs. 5 – vs. 19, Paul goes to great lengths explaining tongues versus prophecy and their attributes, so we will be spending some time in these verses. Verse 5 starts out by Paul stating that the one who prophesies is more important than the one speaking in an unknown tongue unless the one who is speaking in tongues interprets to edify the church. The gift of prophecy and the gift of interpretation of tongues are given by the Holy Spirit to edify the church. It was Paul's desire that everyone would speak in tongues, but his greater desire was that all should prophecy; prophecy being the greater gift. (Just because you give a prophecy does not make you a prophet of the five-fold ministry. Do not confuse the gift with the calling.)

---

[25] NASB

[26] KJV

In vs. 6 through vs. 12 we see that Paul starts by saying how would he benefit the listeners if he came to them speaking in tongues? Those who heard him would not receive any prophecy, or word of knowledge or revelation or doctrine[27], because they would not understand what he was saying.

We see that the Holy Spirit through Paul gives several illustrations of the inabilities of a person to be able to understand an unknown tongue. We see the examples of the musical instruments that if they only play one note how are we to discern the tune that is being played or when we need to prepare to go into battle. If you do not speak with understanding you are talking into the air. It is much like someone who is speaking in their native language, which is foreign to our understanding. We are foreigners to them and them to us. Since we are seeking spiritual gifts we should seek those that edify the church, but not forsaking the gift of tongues. Paul goes on to say that even though he was thankful that he spoke in tongues more than anybody else, when he was around other people he would rather speak with his understanding, so he could edify them with the Word of God. Paul has demon- strated

---

[27] Doctrine, (KJV) Teaching, (NAS) Instruction, (NIV) "The New Strong's Expanded Dictionary of Bible Words" by James Strong, LL.D., S.T.D., p. 1042, n. 1322

that there is a need for both gifts and prophecy being the greater of the two.

We go on to the next six verses, vs. 20 – vs. 25, where Paul NASB tries to instill in the Corinthian Church the need to think like mature adults on Spiritual Gifts and not like children, but to be infants in evil. Then goes on to say, referring to Isaiah 28: 11 & 12 NASB that even though He sent foreigners to His chosen people to share the good news they still did not listen; indicating that the Corinthians' need to take heed to what Paul is saying about Spiritual gifts.

We see the gift of tongues and the gift of prophecy are signs to the believer and the unbeliever. The prior gift is a sign for the unbeliever and the latter gift is a sign for believers. So consequently if an unbeliever enters the sanctuary and hears everybody speaking in tongues he will think that you are all mad, but if he enters and all are prophesying then he will be convicted of his sins and repent and exclaim "God is really among you!" How many church services have you been to that you can say that happened in your presence? I am sad to say it has not happened yet in my life time, but I am looking forward to the day it does! I am not talking about receiving salvation in general; I am talking about people taking turns prophesying and the sinner in their midst receiving salvation and exclaiming out loud, "God is among you."

In verses 26 through 33a Paul (NASB) makes a point on the order of service. He starts by showing us what content should be in the service:

- Praise (& worship)
- A word of instruction
- Revelation knowledge (Preaching!)
- A tongue and an interpretation

All of these must be done for the strengthening (edifying) of the church and the word "all" is all inclusive. If all of these are not happening in the present day church service, then we are limiting God and His Holy Spirit. Are not the signs given by God supposed to follow us[28]?

Paul goes on to say in verses 27 & 28 if a tongue is given during the course of the service there should be an interpretation and no more than three people should give a tongue, also it needs to be done in an orderly fashion, meaning that they should not speak at the same time or disrupting the order of service. If there is no interpreter then the person speaking in tongues should keep quietly to him-self and speak to God only.

Now verses 29 through 38 do not pertain to our subject matter, so we are going to glean just a few things for continuity. In verse

---

[28] Mark 16: 17 & 18 NASB

33 we see that God is not the author of confusion, but He is a God of peace and that means when we come together as the body of Christ everything should be done in an orderly and peaceful manner; it also means that if God is not the author of confusion we know who is and that would be Satan.[29]

In the last two verses we are to desire the gift of prophesy and not forbid the speaking in tongues. Making sure we do everything decently and in order.

Hopefully we now have a better understanding of the gift of tongues, which we know is a gift from the Holy Spirit. The language given is not understood by any man. It is used to speak to God about the unknown (Mysteries). When we use the gift of tongues we build ourselves up (Edify). We do not forbid its use in the church assembly, but when it is used it needs to be interpreted. If no interpretation is given then the person giving the tongue should keep to himself. The gift of tongues increases one's prayer life exponentially. It shows that we are to use the gift of tongues as the Holy Spirit directs and above all it should be used in today's church.

In review we will see how to receive the baptism of the Holy Spirit in the next chapter.

---

[29] [You might want to do a study on this passage at a later time.]

CHAPTER 03

RECEIVING BAPTISM OF
THE HOLY SPIRIT

After going through all of this; this is the simplest thing to do. As a church body you have your Senior Pastor set a date and time to meet after much prayer and fasting; then wait upon the Holy Spirit. Another way is to invite a Spirit filled pastor or one of the other five fold ministry to come and lay hands on each individual, with aforementioned preparation. You can use any other way that has been described in this thesis; or described in the Holy Scriptures.

The main point is as Christians we need to be baptized by the Holy Spirit as well as water baptism.

We will now take a look at my personal account of receiving the baptism of the Holy Spirit.

CHAPTER 04

MY BAPTISM OF THE HOLY SPIRIT

If you would have told me back in the year of 1972, around December, right after I had gotten out of the Air Force that I was going to receive the Baptism of the Holy Spirit I would have told you that you were crazy. At that time I was going to an American Baptist Church and the Baptism of the Holy Spirit was the furthest thing from my mind. When I returned to my home church I found that we had a new pastor. Now unknown to me this pastor was associating himself and our church with Melodyland (No longer exists), which was across from Disneyland in Anaheim, California. The Pastor of Melodyland was Ralph Wilkerson and he was not the brother of David Wilkerson as I was led to believe. They were associates however and David did minister at Melodyland on several occasions. I bring this up only because I was not sure which Wilkerson came to our church to usher in the Holy Spirit, [30]but I digress.

In the year of 1973 our church was growing and the pastor was helping us to understand the functioning of the Holy Spirit.

Now I am not good with dates, so I cannot give an exact date when Pastor Ralph Wilkerson came to our church, but I do remember the day; it was a special Saturday evening service, because we never met on Saturdays and we will review that evening event later.

I remember the event very well because in preparation of this event I fasted for three days, because I wanted to make sure I was hearing from the Lord. Now this was especially taboo for me, because if I did not eat at regular intervals I would get a very bad headache, sick to my stomach, and become totally bed ridden until I received sustenance to regain my strength. Two of The three days I had to go to work and do the job that required physical labor. I believe that Jesus said that man does not live by bread alone, but by every word that proceedeth out of the mouth of God[31], so the only thing I brought for lunch was my Bible. We were union, so we had two breaks and a lunch. Now on our first break I opened the Word and feasted on it. Surprisingly enough the hunger pains

---

[30] Information retrieved from Wikipedia - Online

[31] Matthew 4: 4 (KJV)

went away. At lunch time I was really hungry and I did not know for sure if the Word of God would be enough, (I was not too well learned on the Word of God; still a baby Christian for more years than I want to admit.) and through the entire lunch break I read the Word. Guess what! The hunger pains went away and did not return. No headache, no upset stomach, and no weakness. To say God performed a miracle in my life is putting it mildly. The second day of work was the same miracle. God met my spiritual needs as well as my physical needs.

The day of the event had arrived, and I was really looking forward to receiving something from the Lord! Mind you as a baby Christian I still had doubts about if this was real and if it was for me.

We were all assembled in the chapel, which was across from the main sanctuary, and we proceeded with the service. The first to receive the Baptism of the Holy Spirit was the senior pastor then his wife and so it went on. Pastor Wilkerson laid hands on people and they received the Baptism of the Holy Spirit. The evidence of tongues was not prevalent at the time of the service, (Though I am sure some did receive the gift.) because as Baptists we did not believe in the gift of tongues, in fact some thought it was evil, but the evidence of receiving the Baptism of the Holy Spirit was evident by being slain in the Spirit. Now I know that some of my Pentecostal friends will have issue with this, but remember we were Baptist and who are we to limit God? Now through the whole service I was spreading my fleece[32], as it were, to God by asking Him if He wanted me to have this He would have Pastor Wilkerson call me forward to receive the Baptism of the Holy Spirit. Now the service was winding down and I was getting concerned that I was going to be left out; in fact Pastor Wilkerson was in his closing statements. I earnestly and desperately prayed again that Pastor.

Wilkerson call me forward. And guess what? He did! I was about half way there when the Holy Spirit hit me like a ton of bricks. I could feel myself falling backwards as if in slow motion. I do not remember hitting the floor, which was a tiled concrete floor, and I was not hurt in any way, but when I became aware of my surroundings again I could feel the presence of God like I never felt His presence before. It was a totally awesome experience, which I am thankful to God for allowing me this experience. I was now a complete Baptist I had received both Baptisms. (How ironic is that?) Without the Baptism of the Holy Spirit I would not be the minister that I am today; in fact I could not be His minister.

Now my Pentecostal friends would tell you that you have received the Baptism of the Holy Spirit by the evidence of speaking

---

[32] Judges 6: 36 – 40 (NASB)

in tongues. [33][34](This statement is true.) However I did not speak in tongues, when I received my Baptism. You have to remember I was going to a Baptist Church and we did not believe in the gift of tongues. I was an Assistant Pastor for many years, in two different churches, before I received the gift of tongues (I wish I was not so bullheaded); yet I ministered to the people in the Spirit, for that is the only way to minister; allowing God to speak though you by His' Holy Spirit.[35]

God is a gentleman He will not force His gifts upon you. He will wait for you to change your way of thinking (Your Attitude), by learning about Him through His' Holy Word and remember God likes thinking outside the box, because what looks impossible to man is possible for God[36]. All of this was said so we do not have to force someone to speak in tongues to receive the Baptism of the Holy Spirit, but one should receive the gift of tongues down the road of life, because that is one of the signs of being a Christian [37]and the gift of tongues is needed in self edification and the full worship of God.

In review we see if you earnestly seek something from God that

---

[33] Acts 2: 3 & 4 (NASB)

[34] Acts 10: 44 – 46 (NASB)

[35] Mark 13: 11 (NASB)

[36] Mark 10: 27 (NASB)

[37] Mark 16: 17 (NASB)

He wants you to have, then through fasting and prayer (God will bless you whether you fast or not) He will honor you by giving it to you. We also see that the gift of tongues is needed in a Christian's life to be a complete Christian and to have a fuller experience in worshiping God. We, also, need not force a gift on someone if they are not ready to receive it. I hope by my sharing my experience of receiving the Baptism of the Holy Spirit; it will help the reader of this thesis to (NASB) understand the importance of receiving The Baptism of the Holy Spirit and speaking in tongues in today's church.

CHAPTER 05

THE FRUIT THE HOLY SPIRIT

We should probably have a better understanding of the Holy Spirit of God since we understand we need to be baptized into the Holy Spirit.

But the fruit of the Spirit is love, joy, peace, longsuffering, gentleness, goodness, faith, meekness, temperance: against such there is no law. [38] As you can see it requires a lot of words to describe the fruit of the Spirit and if you look ahead a few scriptures you will see it requires even more words to describe the fruit of man's spirit (The sinful nature, which obviously shows that man, has a lot of sin to overcome by the grace of God).

We are focusing on the words required to describe the fruit of the Holy Spirit. The first word is love; this is the agape [39] type love God has for us. When we accept Christ as our Lord and Savior

---

[38] Galatians 5: 22 & 23 (KJV)

[39] The New Strong's Expanded Dictionary of Bible Words p. 907, #26 (8)

this fruit is instilled in us as the Holy Spirit enters our lives. We are not immediately aware of this love, to its full extent, but as we grow in Christ through the hearing and the study of God's Word we will cultivate that love and it will be seen in us by others. This is the type of love that goes beyond our love for our family, brothers, and sisters in Christ it goes to the point of loving our enemies, so this love is un-conditional.[40][41]

The next word to describe the fruit of the Holy Spirit is Joy. Joy in this instance is the feelings or peace one gets when in the presence of God's Holy Spirit. [42]As we know the joy of the Lord is our strength. [43]Remember when you are in trials and tribulations consider them as joy for while Christ was on this earth He went through trials during His ministry. [44]The word that comes after joy is peace, which implies quietness and resting in your spirit through His Holy Spirit; that peace which He gives that passes beyond our understanding. [45][46]A peace that no matter what the

---

[40] Matthew 5: 44 – 48 (NASB)

[41] Un-conditional – observation of dealing with God's Love to mankind

[42] The New Strong's Expanded Dictionary of Bible Words p. 1450, #5479 (1)

[43] Nehemiah 8: 10 (NASB)

[44] James 1: 2 – 4 (NASB)

[45] John 14: 27 (NASB)

[46] Philippians 4: 7 (KJV)

circumstances; you can be in a near death experience and you have a calm within you that you otherwise would not have.

Our next word is longsuffering, which means being patient and enduring in the face of suffering or difficulty. [47]Simply put, as Holy Spirit filled Christians we stay calm in the time of crisis, in the times of turmoil, and be able to wait upon the Lord to get us through it.

The next word to describe the fruit of the Holy Spirit is gentleness. This word is defined as the act of gentleness. It is acting (Participating) in tenderness. [48]Not being harsh to someone; as the Word says: A gentle (Soft) word turns away wrath.[49]

Another word to describe the fruit of the Holy Spirit is goodness. This is applied as a kind disposition to others; the example given is Jesus' attitude towards the penitent woman (Luke 7: 37 – 50 EXB). [50]There are a lot of people that have goodness as a virtue, but without Christ in their lives they are condemned to the final judgment and eternal separation from God being cast into the lake of fire forever.[51]

The word that comes after goodness is faithful- ness. Faithfulness

---

[47] Encarta Dictionary – Microsoft Word

[48] The New Strong's Expanded Dictionary of Bible Words p. 1458, #5544 (3)

[49] Proverbs 15: 1(NASB)

[50] The New Strong's Expanded Dictionary of Bible Words p. 906, # 19 (2 (A))

[51] Revelations 20: 11 – 15 (NASB)

is the virtue of being dependable and loyal; an example of that is attending church every Sunday without fail. Another example is giving of your tithes and offerings, without grumbling; in fact cheerfully in recognition of your love for Christ.

The next to the last word we will cover is gentleness. This is a virtue that pervades and penetrates the whole nature that mellows anything harsh and austere. Gentleness is the virtue that is gentle, charming, and calm, suited to the company of all good people, attracting their friendship, delightful in encouragement and moderate in manners. [52]You see the importance of the Holy Spirit infusing our spirit, supernaturally, with gentleness; allowing the harshness and severity of dealing with people to be softened.

The final word to describe the fruit of the Spirit is self-control. Self-control is the ability to control your own behavior, especially in terms of reactions and impulses. [53]This means that you are able to keep your anger under control, also keeping your lusts and desires under control, and keeping your pride in check.

We see that as a Christian the fruit of the Holy Spirit should be exemplary in our life, seen by all. Now that we have looked at the fruit of the Spirit; let us look at the gifts of the Holy Spirit.

---

[52] The New Strong's Expanded Dictionary of Bible Words p. 1456 # 5544

[53] From Encarta Dictionary – Microsoft Word

CHAPTER 06

THE GIFTS OF THE HOLY SPIRIT

Now there are several gifts of the Spirit. We will be focusing on those found in the book of Ephesians Chapter 4, the book of I Corinthians Chapter 12, and the book of Romans Chapter 12.

The first gifts we will look at are the gifts given to the Church, the body of Christ (I included the gifts to the church, because they are controlled by the Holy Spirit):

And He gave some to be apostles; and some, prophets; and some, evangelist; some pastors and teachers; for the perfecting of the saints, for the work of the ministry, for the edifying of the body of Christ.[54]

You can see that Christ gave gifts to the church to keep the church functioning, and in this passage they are given in their importance. The first gift listed is the apostle, which has been

---

[54] Ephesians 4: 11 – 12 (KJV)

neglected, abused, miss- represented, and even ignored. Some churches say a man can be in the "office" of the apostle in that while he is building a church he is in that office, and then when he starts ministering in that church he is pastor/teacher. Apparently according to this view one is not able to be an apostle for any length of time.

The apostles of old (The first apostles) had to establish a church because there were no churches, but once they were established, then they could minister to the various churches as needed. The task of the apostle has not changed. He is to minister to the various churches as God directs and yes if needed establish a church in a community. He is to be all things to all people. [55]At one church he may need to be a prophet to another an evangelist, and another a pastor/teacher; he may have to be everything to one church. It is what is needed at the time and God will show the apostle what it is. In Paul's letters to the churches, he was addressing what was needed at that church. We have the privilege to read those letters and to grow as a church, but I digress a little. You do not wake up one day and poof you are an apostle. The first apostles received extensive training from Jesus before they were appointed by Him to be apostles[56]; except for Paul who received man's education

---

[55] I Corinthians 9: 22 (NASB)

[56] Luke 6: 12 & 16 (NASB)

of God's Word, which Jesus used for His glory[57]. We need true apostles to strengthen the local churches and unite them in spirit and in truth. As you can see Jesus Christ continues to choose His apostles. Holy men of God will verify them to be just that, Apostles. We can see then that the apostle is a gift from Christ to the Church. The next gift, which will be discussed, is a Prophet.

Jesus calls a person to be a prophet, holy men of God will confirm this calling, and we will know them by their fruits[58]. Prophets are given to prophesy to the Church Body and to the individual, which exhort, confirm, and express past and future happenings; confirming what is already in an individual's heart. As I have mentioned earlier in this thesis just because you give a prophecy does not make you a prophet. Again Christ calls you to this calling and holy men confirm this to be true. If you hold this position in the Church like the apostle you need to be totally grounded in the Word of God. Two examples of prophecy are as follows:

1. Jesus saw Nathanael coming to him, and saith of him, Behold an Israelite indeed, in whom is no guile!

---

[57] Acts 9: 10 – 16 (NASB)

[58] Matthew 7: 15 & 16 (NASB)

Nathanael saith unto him, Whence knowest thou me? Jesus answered and said unto him, Before that Philip called thee, when thou wast under the fig tree, I saw thee.[59]

2. Then He took the twelve aside and said to them, "Behold, we are going up to Jerusalem, and all things which are written through the prophets about the Son of Man will be accomplished. For He will be handed over to the Gentiles, and will be mocked and mistreated and spit upon, and after they have scourged Him, they will kill Him; and the third day He will rise again."[60]

In the first prophecy Jesus exhorts Nathanael in that there was no guile in him, which means he was an honest man and also confirms what Nathanael already knew. Jesus also told him of his recent past that he was sitting under a fig tree when his brother came to him to tell him about Jesus.

The second prophecy is about Jesus' near future in that He was going to be turned over to the gentiles and be spat upon, beaten, whipped, killed, and He would rise on the third day.

I used Jesus' prophecies because He is our perfect example. Granted he has a connection with the Father we will only have

---

[59] John 1: 47 & 48 (KJV) by public domain

[60] Luke 18: 31 – 33 (NASB)

when we see Jesus face to face, but Today's prophet needs to be steeped into the Holy Spirit, so he can, discern, be assured that it is the Holy Spirit speaking and not him. (This is accomplished though constant meditation, fasting and prayer.)

Like apostles there are a lot of false prophets. You need to be sure that what they prophesy is in line with God's Word.

The third appointment or gift is given to the Church is the evangelist; in the Greek (Ευαγγελιστής, yoo-ang- ghel-is-tace') "preacher of the gospel", [61]which means that they go around and preach the Good News. In the church today they seem to have the obligation of bringing revival to the churches, and to go into the mission field. Today when we say evangelist we think of John Wesley, Billy Graham, Oral Roberts, Pat Robertson, Jerry Falwell, and others too numerous to list. [62]They shared the Good News to the masses; with God watching His Word to perform it [63]and brought forth much fruit from the fields of the lost[64]. We are all called to evangelize in the Great Commission[65], but Christ gives a special anointing on the evangelist; in that the gift of healing, sighs and confirmations are with him in his ministry.

---

[61] 2099 in The New Strong's Expanded Dictionary of the Bible

[62] Biography.com/ "Famous Evangelists"

[63] Jeremiah 1: 9 – 12 (NASB)

[64] Matthew 9: 37 (NASB)

[65] Matthew 28: 16 – 20 (NASB)

The next two gifts we will look at together. The reason these two gifts are being examined together is a pastor is usually a teacher too, because in the process of preaching some learning is achieved by the listener and during Bible studies the pastor teaches, however you do not need to be a pastor to be a teacher. Let us look first at the pastor and his position in the Church. The pastor, like the first three are appointed by Christ, oversees the local church. He is the mainstay of the Church. He is the one who feeds the local flock. He is to seek God first then minister to the people; in other words he serves God not the people. A wise pastor appoints deacons, according to God's Word[66], to help the local body of Christ and he or she, also, helps the pastor run the church as smoothly as possible, so he can devote his time with Christ the author and finisher of our faith. The [67]pastor's wife is sometimes, unofficially, is assigned as a deaconess due to the lack of church members and after the church has grown we forget to decommission them, so that they can support their husbands in other ways.

A teacher, appointed by Christ, is an intricate part of the local church, because according to scripture: "My people perish

---

[66] I Timothy 3: 8 – 13 (NASB)

[67] Hebrews 12: 2 (KJV)

or destroyed for the lack of knowledge", [68]to give the necessary knowledge to the body of Christ, which enables the body to grow and mature in their daily walk in Christ; adding to knowledge wisdom, so the body can use the knowledge that they have received.

We need to be careful when we assign people in positions in the church. We need to make sure that the person is indeed called by Christ to fill that position and not of our own desire to fill a vacancy or to create a position. We have covered the fivefold ministry; we will now look at the rest of the gifts of the Holy Spirit.

The next groups of gifts we will look at are found in the book of I Corinthians 12: 8 – 10 NASB[69]. The first two gifts work hand in hand, which are the gift of giving a word of wisdom, and the second is the word of knowledge. The fist gift mentioned is the word of wisdom this gift supplements the gift of knowledge, in that it explains how to put the word of knowledge to use. The word of knowledge is the ability to enlighten the hearer with the word of God - to give them the understanding of God's Word.

The next gift is the gift of faith; it is a faith that is unwavering; that will not falter. This is the faith that no matter the circumstances

---

[68] Hosea 4: 6 (NASB)

[69] NASB

they know God will get them through; that God will perform a miracle on their behalf.

They don't just pray a simple prayer; they fast and pray, if necessary with their faces to the ground. They take God serious and believe in the Word of God; that they can move mountains.[70]

The working of miracles [71]is a gift that The Spirit gives to show the power of God; that He is real and living. There is the miracle of healing (The blind see, the spinal cord made whole, the lame walk, etcetera, and etcetera). The miracle of avoiding death; Thrown from a car unscathed, live through a tornado or hurricane that demolished a house, etcetera, and etcetera. There are other types of miracles, which are insurmountable to mention.

The next gift listed is prophecy, which we have already covered this gift in length; the gift that follows is the distinguishing (discerning) of spirits. This gift helps us to know which spirit is at work holy or demonic. If demonic we can discern whether it is the spirit of depression, infirmity, muteness, and etcetera, so we can cast out or bind or loosen whatever is called for in any particular circumstance. On a side note; when you fight the spiritual war you better have the full armor of God on.[72]

---

[70] Matthew 17: 19 – 21

[71] KJV

[72] Ephesians 10 – 17

The last two gifts are various tongues and interpretation of tongues, which we have already covered. That brings us to the last group of gifts found in Romans 12: 6 – 8 NASB[73].

In this last passage some of the gifts have already been covered and will not be covered again here. The first gift that is being covered is service; this gift can be spiritual in that a person with this gift will do more than go out of their way to serve you. They are ready to serve at a moment's notice. They will serve where ever they are needed.

The next gift is exhortation, which means recommend or advise[74]; this gift is used to edify or to build-up and motivate.

The next gift is giving, which is giving with great generosity; sometimes to their being hurt. The saying, "They will give you the shirt off their back" comes to mind. Just saying they are philanthropic in giving.

The next gift is leading; some of the great leaders have or had this gift. Paul and Peter are two good examples, who had the gift of leading.

The last gift is mercy, which is an awesome gift. This gift allows you to have compassion for someone when nobody else will.

We will now cover the conclusions that have been formed.

---

[73] NASB

[74] The Strong's Expanded Dictionary of Bible Words, p 1290 #3867

CHAPTER 07

CONCLUSIONS

We see that it is still necessary to receive the Baptism of the Holy Spirit in today's church; as the body of Christ or as an individual. The way we receive that baptism can happen anytime, anywhere, and any method that God sees fit. We see that when we are baptized in the Holy Spirit we are able to speak in tongues, and we are able to speak with boldness and power making us His witnesses that He wants us to be.

We covered the gift of tongues verses the gift of prophecy and that each gift has its place in the church. The gift of tongues is for the individual for self-edification; while the gift of tongues is for the church only if it is interpreted and the gift of tongues is not to be excluded from the church. We see how we can receive the Holy Spirit through the Pastor of the church as a whole or a guest speaker or individually by laying on of hands.

We have a personal account of how I received the baptism of

the Holy Spirit and what I experienced; giving us insight of one of the ways of experiencing the baptism of the Holy Spirit.

The fruit of the Holy Spirit is all encompassing our spirit, so others can see Christ in us and to glorify His name.

The gifts of Christ to the Church (The fivefold ministry) are to be present in today's church and the other spiritual gifts are what He uses to glorify God (Jesus Christ.); the Holy Spirit distributes them as He pleases. There continues to be a manifestation of the Holy Spirit's gifts in today's church.

Printed in the United States
By Bookmasters